SIMPLE 1·2·3™

Chicken

pil

Publications International, Ltd.

Favorite Brand Name Recipes at www.fbnr.com

Microwave Cooking: Microwave ovens vary in wattage. Use the cooking times as guidelines and check for doneness before adding more time.

Preparation/Cooking Times: Preparation times are based on the approximate amount of time required to assemble the recipe before cooking, baking, chilling or serving. These times include preparation steps such as measuring, chopping and mixing. The fact that some preparations and cooking can be done simultaneously is taken into account. Preparation of optional ingredients and serving suggestions is not included.

Contents

Soups, Stews & Chilis

Sopa de Lima

2 tablespoons olive oil
2 pounds chicken thighs
   and legs
1 cup chopped yellow
   onion
2 cloves garlic, minced
6 cups water
1 cup seeded and
   chopped tomatoes
1 jalapeño pepper,
   minced*
1 tablespoon chili powder
1 teaspoon ground cumin
1 teaspoon dried oregano
3 tablespoons lime juice
2 teaspoons salt or to
   taste
½ cup chopped fresh
   cilantro
¼ cup finely chopped
   radishes
   Lime wedges

*Jalapeño peppers can sting and
irritate the skin; wear rubber gloves
when handling peppers and do not
touch eyes. Wash hands
after handling.

1. Heat a Dutch oven over medium-high heat until hot. Add oil and chicken; cook on both sides until browned, about 4 minutes total. Remove to plate.

2. Add onion and garlic to Dutch oven. Reduce heat to medium; cook 3 to 4 minutes or until onions are translucent. Increase heat to high, add water, and bring to a boil. Add reserved chicken, tomatoes, jalapeño, chili powder, cumin and oregano. Bring just to a boil, reduce heat, cover tightly; simmer 1 hour or until chicken is falling off bone. Remove chicken with slotted spoon and cool slightly; remove meat from bone, shred, and return to Dutch oven with lime juice and salt.

3. Combine cilantro and radishes. Serve soup in bowls; garnish with cilantro mixture and lime wedges. *Makes 6 servings*

Chicken and Black Bean Chili

1 pound boneless skinless chicken thighs, cut into 1-inch chunks
2 teaspoons chili powder
2 teaspoons ground cumin
¾ teaspoon salt
1 green bell pepper, diced
1 small onion, chopped
3 cloves garlic, minced
1 can (14.5 ounces) diced tomatoes, undrained
1 cup chunky salsa
1 can (16 ounces) black beans, rinsed and drained
Sour cream, diced ripe avocado, shredded Cheddar cheese, sliced green onions, chopped fresh cilantro, tortilla or corn chips for topping (optiona)

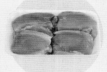

Slow Cooker Directions

1. Coat slow cooker with cooking spray. Combine chicken, chili powder, cumin and salt in slow cooker, tossing to coat. Add bell pepper, onion and garlic; mix well. Stir in tomatoes and salsa. Cover and cook 5 to 6 hours on LOW or 2½ to 3 hours on HIGH, or until chicken is no longer pink in center.

2. Turn heat to high; stir in beans. Cover and cook 5 to 10 minutes or until beans are heated through. Ladle into shallow bowls; serve with desired toppings. *Makes 4 servings*

Chicken Stew

Slow Cooker Directions

1. Combine chicken, tomatoes with juice, potatoes, okra and onion in slow cooker. Cover; cook on LOW 6 to 8 hours or until potatoes are tender.

2. Add corn, ketchup and barbecue sauce. Cover; cook on HIGH 30 minutes. *Makes 6 servings*

Serving Suggestion: Serve this stew with breadsticks and sliced tomatoes on a bed of lettuce, and your meal is complete.

4 to 5 cups chopped cooked chicken (about 5 boneless skinless chicken breasts)
1 can (28 ounces) whole tomatoes, undrained
2 large potatoes, cut into 1-inch pieces
½ pound okra, sliced
1 large onion, chopped
1 can (14 ounces) cream-style corn
½ cup ketchup
½ cup barbecue sauce

Soups, Stews & Chilis

1 can (49½ ounces) fat-
    free reduced-sodium
    chicken broth *or*
3 cans (14½ ounces
    each) fat-free
    reduced-sodium
    chicken broth plus
    6 ounces of water
1 cup grated carrots
½ cup sliced green onions
½ cup diced red bell
    pepper
½ cup frozen green peas
1 seedless cucumber
12 chicken tenders (about
    1 pound)
½ teaspoon white pepper

Main-Dish Chicken Soup

1. Place broth in large 4-quart Dutch oven. Bring to a boil over high heat. Add carrots, green onions, bell pepper and peas. Return to a boil. Reduce heat and simmer 3 minutes.

2. Meanwhile, cut ends off cucumber and discard. Using vegetable peeler, start at top and make long, noodle-like strips of cucumber. Slice remaining cucumber pieces thinly with knife. Add cucumber strips to Dutch oven; cook 2 minutes over low heat.

3. Add chicken tenders and white pepper; simmer 5 minutes or until chicken is browned.   *Makes 6 servings*

Serving Suggestion: Serve this soup with a small mixed green salad.

Soups, Stews & Chilis

Black and White Chili

1. Spray large saucepan with cooking spray; heat over medium heat until hot. Add chicken and onion; cook and stir over medium to medium-high heat 5 to 8 minutes or until chicken is browned.

2. Stir beans, tomatoes with juice and seasoning mix into saucepan; bring to a boil. Reduce heat to low; simmer, uncovered, 10 minutes. Serve over rice, if desired. *Makes 6 servings*

Prep and Cook Time: *30 minutes*

Nonstick cooking spray
1 pound chicken tenders, cut into ¾-inch pieces
1 cup coarsely chopped onion
1 can (15½ ounces) Great Northern beans, rinsed and drained
1 can (15 ounces) black beans, rinsed and drained
1 can (14½ ounces) Mexican-style stewed tomatoes, undrained
2 tablespoons Texas-style chili powder seasoning mix
Hot cooked rice (optional)

Chicken Tortilla Soup

2 large ripe avocados, halved and pitted
4 teaspoons TABASCO® brand Green Pepper Sauce, divided
½ teaspoon salt or to taste
3 (14½-ounce) cans chicken broth
3 boneless skinless chicken breast halves (about 1 pound)
2 tablespoons uncooked rice
1 large tomato, seeded and chopped
½ cup chopped onion
¼ cup finely chopped cilantro
Tortilla chips
½ cup (2 ounces) shredded Monterey Jack cheese

Scoop out avocado into medium bowl and mash with fork. Add 1½ teaspoons TABASCO® Green Pepper Sauce and salt; blend gently but thoroughly. Set aside.

Heat chicken broth to boiling in 4-quart saucepan. Add chicken breast halves; reduce heat and cook until chicken is opaque. Remove chicken and cut into bite-size pieces. Add rice and cook about 15 minutes or until tender. Return chicken to saucepan. Just before serving, stir in tomato, onion, cilantro and remaining 2½ teaspoons TABASCO® Green Pepper Sauce.

To serve, break small handful of tortilla chips into bottom of each bowl. Ladle soup over tortilla chips. Top with cheese and 1 rounded tablespoon avocado mixture. Serve immediately with additional TABASCO® Green Pepper Sauce, if desired. *Makes 8 servings*

Soups, Stews & Chilis

Sausage and Chicken Gumbo

1. Heat oil in large saucepan. Add bell pepper; cook and stir over medium-high heat 2 to 3 minutes. Add chicken; cook and stir about 2 minutes or until browned. Add sausage; cook and stir 2 minutes or until browned. Add broth; scrape up any browned bits from bottom of saucepan.

2. Add tomatoes, green onions, bay leaf, basil, black pepper and red pepper flakes. Simmer 15 minutes. Remove and discard bay leaf. Garnish each serving with lemon wedge, if desired.   *Makes 6 servings*

1 tablespoon canola oil
1 red bell pepper, chopped
1 pound boneless skinless chicken thighs, trimmed of fat and cut into 1-inch pieces
1 package (12 ounces) chili flavor chicken sausage, sliced ½ inch thick
½ cup chicken broth
1 can (28 ounces) crushed tomatoes with roasted garlic
¼ cup finely chopped green onions
1 bay leaf
½ teaspoon dried basil
½ teaspoon black pepper
¼ to ½ teaspoon red pepper flakes
6 lemon wedges (optional)

Soups, Stews & Chilis

Chunky Chicken and Vegetable Soup

1 tablespoon canola oil
1 boneless skinless
    chicken breast
    (4 ounces), diced
½ cup chopped green bell
    pepper
½ cup thinly sliced celery
2 green onions, sliced
2 cans (14½ ounces each)
    chicken broth
1 cup water
½ cup sliced carrots
2 tablespoons cream
1 tablespoon finely
    chopped fresh parsley
¼ teaspoon dried thyme
⅛ teaspoon black pepper

1. Heat oil in large saucepan over medium heat. Add chicken; cook and stir 4 to 5 minutes or until no longer pink in center. Add bell pepper, celery and onions. Cook and stir 7 minutes or until vegetables are tender.

2. Add broth, water, carrots, cream, parsley, thyme and black pepper. Simmer 10 minutes or until carrots are tender.

Makes 4 servings

Confetti Chicken Chili

1. Brown chicken in large skillet over medium-high heat, stirring to break up meat. Drain fat.

2. Add remaining ingredients to saucepan. Bring to a boil. Reduce heat to low and simmer 15 minutes.   *Makes 5 servings*

Prep & Cook Time: *30 minutes*

1 pound 90% fat-free ground chicken
1 large onion, chopped
2 cans (about 14 ounces each) fat-free reduced-sodium chicken broth
1 can (15 ounces) Great Northern beans, rinsed and drained
2 carrots, chopped
1 medium green bell pepper, chopped
2 plum tomatoes, chopped
1 jalapeño pepper,* finely chopped (optional)
2 teaspoons chili powder
½ teaspoon ground red pepper

*Jalapeño peppers can sting and irritate the skin; wear rubber gloves when handling peppers and do not touch eyes. Wash hands after handling.

Tuscan Chicken with White Beans

1 large fresh fennel bulb (about ¾ pound)
1 teaspoon olive oil
½ pound boneless skinless chicken thighs, cut into ¾-inch pieces
1 teaspoon dried rosemary
½ teaspoon black pepper
1 can (14½ ounces) no-salt-added stewed tomatoes
1 can (about 14 ounces) fat-free reduced-sodium chicken broth
1 can (15 ounces) cannellini beans, rinsed and drained
Hot pepper sauce (optional)

1. Cut off and reserve ¼ cup chopped feathery fennel tops. Chop bulb into ½-inch pieces. Heat oil in large saucepan over medium heat. Add chopped fennel bulb; cook 5 minutes, stirring occasionally.

2. Sprinkle chicken with rosemary and black pepper; add to saucepan. Cook and stir 2 minutes. Add tomatoes with juice and chicken broth; bring to a boil. Cover; simmer 10 minutes. Stir in beans; simmer, uncovered, 15 minutes or until chicken is no longer pink in center and sauce thickens. Season to taste with hot pepper sauce, if desired. Ladle into 4 shallow bowls; top with reserved fennel tops.

Makes 4 servings

Prep Time: *15 minutes*
Cook Time: *35 minutes*

Soups, Stews & Chilis

Chicken & Orzo Soup

1. Spray medium saucepan with cooking spray. Heat over medium-high heat. Add chicken. Cook and stir 2 to 3 minutes or until no longer pink in center. Remove from saucepan; set aside.

2. In same saucepan, combine broth, water, green onion, orzo, ginger and turmeric. Bring to a boil. Reduce heat and simmer, covered, 8 to 10 minutes or until orzo is tender. Stir in chicken and lemon juice; cook until hot. Season to taste with pepper.

3. Ladle into serving bowls. Sprinkle with additional green onion, if desired. *Makes 2 servings*

Nonstick olive oil cooking spray
3 ounces boneless skinless chicken breast, cut into bite-size pieces
1 can (14½ ounces) fat-free reduced-sodium chicken broth
1 cup water
⅓ cup sliced green onion
¼ cup uncooked orzo pasta
1 teaspoon grated fresh ginger
⅛ teaspoon ground turmeric
2 teaspoons lemon juice
Dash black pepper
Sliced green onion (optional)

Chicken & White Bean Stew

1 tablespoon olive oil

2 medium carrots, sliced
   (about 2 cups)

1 medium onion, thinly
   sliced

2 cloves garlic, finely
   chopped

1 tablespoon balsamic
   vinegar

1 pound boneless, skinless
   chicken breast halves
   or thighs, cut into
   chunks

1 jar (1 pound 10 ounces)
   RAGÚ® Old World
   Style® Pasta Sauce

2 cans (15 ounces each)
   cannellini or white
   kidney beans, rinsed
   and drained

Pinch crushed red
   pepper flakes
   (optional)

In 12-inch skillet, heat olive oil over medium heat and cook carrots, onion and garlic, stirring occasionally, 5 minutes or until vegetables are tender. Stir in vinegar and cook 1 minute. Remove vegetables; set aside.

In same skillet, thoroughly brown chicken over medium-high heat. Return vegetables to skillet. Stir in Ragú Old World Style Pasta Sauce, beans and red pepper flakes. Bring to a boil over high heat. Reduce heat to medium and simmer covered, stirring occasionally, 15 minutes or until chicken is thoroughly cooked. Garnish, if desired, with fresh parsley and serve with toasted Italian bread. *Makes 6 servings*

Soups, Stews & Chilis

Thai Noodle Soup

1. Break noodles into pieces. Cook noodles according to package directions (discard flavor packet). Drain and set aside.

2. Cut chicken tenders into ½-inch pieces. Combine chicken broth and chicken tenders in large saucepan or Dutch oven; bring to a boil over medium heat. Cook 2 minutes or until chicken is no longer pink in center.

3. Add carrot, snow peas, green onion, garlic and ginger. Reduce heat to low; simmer 3 minutes. Add cooked noodles and cilantro; heat through. Serve soup with lime wedges.   *Makes 4 servings*

Prep and Cook Time: *15 minutes*

1 package (3 ounces)
    ramen noodles
¾ pound chicken tenders
2 cans (about 14 ounces
    each) chicken broth
¼ cup shredded carrot
¼ cup frozen snow peas
2 tablespoons thinly
    sliced green onion
½ teaspoon minced garlic
¼ teaspoon ground ginger
3 tablespoons chopped
    fresh cilantro
½ lime, cut into 4 wedges

Cajun Chili

1. Lightly brown sausage in large skillet over medium-high heat. Add chicken, onion and cayenne pepper; cook until browned. Drain.

2. Stir in remaining ingredients. Cook 5 minutes, stirring occasionally.

Makes 4 servings

Prep and Cook Time: *20 minutes*

6 ounces spicy sausage links, sliced

4 boneless, skinless chicken thighs, cut into cubes

1 medium onion, chopped

⅛ teaspoon cayenne pepper

1 can (15 ounces) black-eyed peas or kidney beans, drained

1 can (14½ ounces) DEL MONTE® Diced Tomatoes with Zesty Mild Green Chilies

1 medium green bell pepper, chopped

White Bean Chili

1. Spray large nonstick skillet with cooking spray. Brown chicken in large skillet over medium-high heat, stirring to break up meat. Drain fat.

2. Add celery, onions and garlic to skillet; cook and stir over medium heat 5 to 7 minutes or until tender. Sprinkle with chili powder, cumin, allspice, cinnamon and pepper; cook and stir 1 minute.

3. Return chicken to skillet. Stir in tomatoes with juice, beans and chicken broth; heat to a boil. Reduce heat to low and simmer, uncovered, 15 minutes. Garnish as desired. *Makes 6 servings*

Nonstick cooking spray
1 pound ground chicken
3 cups coarsely chopped celery
1½ cups coarsely chopped onions (about 2 medium)
3 cloves garlic, minced
4 teaspoons chili powder
1½ teaspoons ground cumin
¾ teaspoon ground allspice
¾ teaspoon ground cinnamon
½ teaspoon black pepper
1 can (16 ounces) whole tomatoes, undrained and coarsely chopped
1 can (15½ ounces) Great Northern beans, drained and rinsed
2 cups fat-free reduced-sodium chicken broth

Soups, Stews & Chilis

Hot off the Grill

Chicken Satay

16 chicken tenders (about
    2¼ pounds) or
    4 boneless, skinless
    chicken breasts, cut
    into 16 thin strips
½ cup reduced-sodium soy
    sauce
1 tablespoon vegetable oil
1 onion, chopped
2 cloves garlic, minced
2 teaspoons ground
    ginger
½ cup peanut butter
1½ teaspoons ketchup
½ cup water
¼ teaspoon salt
⅛ teaspoon black pepper

1. Marinate chicken in soy sauce in resealable food storage bag 45 minutes.

2. Meanwhile, heat oil in large nonstick skillet over medium-high heat. Add onion and garlic; cook and stir 5 minutes or until golden brown. Add ginger; stir to blend. Add peanut butter, ketchup, water, salt and pepper; stir to blend.

3. Reduce heat to low. Cook until mixture is heated through. Transfer to blender and purée until smooth. Reserve to use as dipping sauce.

4. Drain chicken and discard soy sauce. Thread chicken strips onto 16 (8-inch) bamboo skewers. Prepare grill for direct grilling. Grill chicken 5 to 6 minutes or until no longer pink in center, turning once.

5. Serve with peanut dipping sauce. *Makes 4 to 6 servings*

Tip: For best results, soak bamboo skewers in water for about 30 minutes before using to make them more pliable and to prevent them from burning.

2 boneless skinless chicken breasts (about 3 ounces each)
¼ cup fresh lime juice
3 tablespoons honey mustard, divided
2 teaspoons olive oil
¼ teaspoon ground cumin
⅛ teaspoon garlic powder
⅛ teaspoon ground red pepper
¾ cup plus 2 tablespoons fat-free, reduced-sodium chicken broth, divided
¼ cup uncooked rice
1 cup broccoli florets
⅓ cup matchstick carrots

1. Rinse chicken. Pat dry with paper towels. Place in resealable food storage bag. Whisk together lime juice, 2 tablespoons mustard, olive oil, cumin, garlic powder and red pepper. Pour over chicken. Seal bag. Marinate in refrigerator 2 hours.

2. Combine ¾ cup chicken broth, rice and remaining 1 tablespoon mustard in small saucepan. Bring to a boil. Reduce heat and simmer, covered, 12 minutes or until rice is almost tender. Stir in broccoli, carrots and remaining 2 tablespoons chicken broth. Cook, covered, 2 to 3 minutes more or until vegetables are crisp-tender and rice is tender.

3. Meanwhile, drain chicken, discard marinade. Prepare grill for direct grilling. Grill chicken over medium coals 10 to 13 minutes or until no longer pink in center. Serve chicken with rice mixture.

Makes 2 servings

Grilled Chicken with Spicy Black Beans & Rice

1. Spray cold grid of grill with nonstick cooking spray. Prepare grill for direct grilling. Rub chicken with jerk seasoning. Grill over medium-hot coals 8 to 10 minutes or until no longer pink in center.

2. Meanwhile, heat oil in medium saucepan or skillet over medium heat. Add bell pepper and chili powder; cook and stir until peppers are soft.

3. Add rice, beans, pimiento and olives to saucepan. Cook about 3 minutes or until hot.

4. Serve bean mixture with chicken. Top bean mixture with onion and cilantro, if desired. Garnish with lime wedges, if desired.

Makes 2 servings

1 boneless skinless chicken breast (about ¼ pound)
½ teaspoon Caribbean jerk seasoning
½ teaspoon olive oil
¼ cup finely diced green bell pepper
2 teaspoons chipotle chili powder
¾ cup hot cooked rice
½ cup rinsed and drained canned black beans
2 tablespoons diced pimiento
1 tablespoon chopped pimiento-stuffed green olives
1 tablespoon chopped onion
1 tablespoon chopped fresh cilantro (optional)
Lime wedges for garnish (optional)

1 pound boneless skinless
   chicken breasts, cut
   into ¾-inch-wide
   strips
2 tablespoons sherry or
   pineapple juice
2 tablespoons reduced-
   sodium soy sauce
1 tablespoon sugar
1 tablespoon peanut oil
½ teaspoon minced garlic
½ teaspoon minced ginger
5 ounces red pearl onions
½ fresh pineapple, cut into
   1-inch wedges

Japanese Yakitori

1. Place chicken in large resealable food storage bag. Combine sherry, soy sauce, sugar, oil, garlic and ginger in small bowl; mix thoroughly to dissolve sugar. Pour into bag with chicken; seal bag and turn to coat thoroughly. Refrigerate 30 minutes or up to 2 hours, turning occasionally. (If using wooden or bamboo skewers, soak them in water 30 minutes to keep from burning.)

2. Meanwhile, place onions in boiling water for 4 minutes; drain and cool in ice water to stop cooking. Cut off root ends and slip off outer skins; set aside.

3. Drain chicken, reserving marinade. Weave chicken accordion-style onto skewers, alternating onions and pineapple with chicken. Brush with reserved marinade; discard remaining marinade.

4. Grill on uncovered grill over medium-hot coals 6 to 8 minutes or until chicken is no longer pink in center, turning once. *Makes 6 servings*

Citrus Marinated Chicken

Combine orange, lemon and lime juices and garlic in a shallow glass dish or large heavy plastic bag. Add chicken; cover dish or close bag. Marinate in refrigerator no more than 2 hours. (Lemon and lime juice will "cook" the chicken if it's left in too long.) Remove chicken from marinade; discard marinade. Season chicken with salt and pepper.

Oil hot grid to help prevent sticking. Grill chicken, on a covered grill, over medium KINGSFORD® Briquets, 6 to 8 minutes until chicken is cooked through, turning once. Serve topped with a dollop of Citrus Tarragon Butter. Serve over couscous, if desired. Garnish, if desired.

Makes 4 servings

Citrus Tarragon Butter

- ½ cup (1 stick) butter, softened
- 1 tablespoon finely chopped fresh tarragon
- 1 tablespoon lemon juice
- 1 tablespoon orange juice
- 1 teaspoon finely grated orange peel
- 1 teaspoon finely grated lemon peel

Beat butter in a small bowl until soft and light. Stir in remaining ingredients. Cover and refrigerate until ready to serve.

Makes about ½ cup

- 1 cup orange juice
- ¼ cup lemon juice
- ¼ cup lime juice
- 2 cloves garlic, pressed or minced
- 4 boneless skinless chicken breast halves
- Salt and black pepper
- Citrus Tarragon Butter (recipe follows)
- Hot cooked couscous with green onion slices and slivered almonds (optional)
- Lemon and lime slices and Italian parsley for garnish

Chicken and Bacon Skewers

2 boneless skinless chicken breasts (about ½ pound)
¼ cup lemon juice
¼ cup soy sauce
2 tablespoons brown sugar
1½ teaspoons lemon pepper
1 teaspoon coarsely ground black pepper
½ pound bacon slices, cut in half crosswise

1. Cut chicken into 1-inch cubes. Combine lemon juice, soy sauce, brown sugar and lemon pepper in large resealable food storage bag; mix well. Remove ¼ cup marinade; set aside. Add chicken to bag; seal. Marinate in refrigerator at least 30 minutes.

2. Sprinkle black pepper over top sides of bacon; gently press in pepper. Fold each slice in half. Remove chicken from bag; discard marinade. Alternately thread chicken and bacon onto skewers.*

3. Grill skewers, turning occasionally, 10 to 15 minutes or until chicken is no longer pink in center and bacon is crisp. Brush several times with reserved marinade. *Makes 2 servings*

If using wooden skewers soak in water 20 to 30 minutes before using to prevent scorching.

Serving Suggestion: Garnish with lemon wedges. Serve as a light entrée or divide and serve as appetizers.

Fajitas on a Stick

Thread chicken, pepper, onion and tomatoes onto skewers, dividing up ingredients equally. Brush heavily and frequently with Tequila Lime Marinade while grilling. Cook chicken 18 minutes or until thoroughly cooked. Place cooked skewer on warm tortilla; remove fajitas from skewer and roll-up tortilla to enclose fajita mixture securely. Serve immediately. *Makes 8 fajitas*

Variation: Also great using LAWRY'S® Mesquite Marinade With Lime Juice.

Prep Time: *20 minutes*
Cook Time: *15 to 18 minutes*

1 pound boneless, skinless chicken breasts, cut into 1-inch pieces
½ green bell pepper, cut into ½-inch pieces
½ onion, sliced into ½-inch slices
16 cherry tomatoes
8 wooden skewers, soaked in water for 30 minutes
1 cup LAWRY'S® Tequila Lime Marinade With Lime Juice
8 fajita-size flour tortillas, warmed to soften

1 cup finely chopped
   white onion
6 finely chopped green
   onions
⅓ cup white wine vinegar
6 cloves garlic, minced
1 habañero pepper,*
   finely chopped
4½ teaspoons olive oil
4½ teaspoons fresh thyme
1 tablespoon ground
   allspice
2 teaspoons sugar
1 teaspoon salt
1 teaspoon ground
   cinnamon
1 teaspoon ground
   nutmeg
1 teaspoon black pepper
½ teaspoon ground red
   pepper
6 boneless skinless
   chicken breasts
   Grilled sweet potatoes
   (optional)

*Habañero peppers can sting and
irritate the skin; wear rubber gloves
when handling peppers and do not
touch eyes. Wash hands after
handling.

Spicy Island Chicken

1. Combine all ingredients except chicken in medium bowl; mix well. Place chicken in resealable food storage bag; add seasoning mixture. Seal bag; turn to coat chicken. Marinate in refrigerator 4 hours or overnight.

2. Spray cold grid with nonstick cooking spray. Adjust grid to 4 to 6 inches above heat. Preheat grill to medium-high heat.

3. Remove chicken from marinade. Grill 5 to 7 minutes per side or until chicken is no longer pink in center, brushing occasionally with marinade. *Do not brush with marinade during last 5 minutes of grilling.* Discard remaining marinade. Garnish and serve with sweet potatoes, if desired.

Makes 6 servings

Grilled Chicken Tostados

1. Place chicken in single layer in shallow glass dish; sprinkle with cumin. Combine orange juice, ¼ cup salsa, 1 tablespoon oil and garlic in small bowl; pour over chicken. Cover; marinate in refrigerator at least 2 hours or up to 8 hours, stirring mixture occasionally.

2. Prepare grill for direct cooking.

3. Drain chicken; reserve marinade. Brush green onions with remaining 2 teaspoons oil. Place chicken and green onions on grid. Grill, covered, over medium-high heat 5 minutes. Brush tops of chicken with half of reserved marinade; turn and brush with remaining marinade. Turn onions. Continue to grill, covered, 5 minutes or until chicken is no longer pink in center and onions are tender. (If onions are browning too quickly, remove before chicken is done.)

4. Meanwhile, combine beans and remaining 2 tablespoons salsa in small saucepan; cook, stirring occasionally, over medium heat until hot.

5. Place tortillas in single layer on grid. Grill, uncovered, 1 to 2 minutes per side or until golden brown. (If tortillas puff up, pierce with tip of knife or flatten by pressing with spatula.)

6. Transfer chicken and onions to cutting board. Slice chicken crosswise into ½-inch strips. Cut onions crosswise into 1-inch-long pieces. Spread tortillas with bean mixture; top with lettuce, chicken, onions, cheese, avocado and tomato, if desired. Sprinkle with cilantro and serve with sour cream, if desired.   *Makes 4 servings*

1 pound boneless skinless chicken breasts
1 teaspoon ground cumin
¼ cup orange juice
¼ cup plus 2 tablespoons salsa, divided
1 tablespoon plus 2 teaspoons vegetable oil, divided
2 cloves garlic, minced
8 green onions
1 can (16 ounces) refried beans
4 (10-inch) *or* **8 (6- to 7-inch)** flour tortillas
2 cups chopped romaine lettuce
1½ cups (6 ounces) shredded Monterey Jack cheese with jalapeño peppers
1 ripe medium avocado, diced (optional)
1 medium tomato, seeded and diced (optional)
Chopped fresh cilantro and sour cream (optional)

Herb Garlic Grilled Chicken

¼ **cup chopped parsley**
1½ **tablespoons minced**
   garlic
4 **teaspoons grated lemon**
   peel
1 **tablespoon chopped**
   fresh mint
1 **chicken (2½ to**
   3 pounds), quartered

Combine parsley, garlic, lemon peel and mint. Loosen skin from breast and thigh portions of chicken quarters by running fingers between skin and meat. Rub some of seasoning mixture evenly over meat under skin, replace skin and rub remaining seasonings over outside of chicken to cover evenly. Arrange medium-hot KINGSFORD® Briquets on one side of covered grill. Place chicken on grid opposite coals. Cover grill and cook chicken 45 to 55 minutes, turning once or twice. Chicken is done when juices run clear. *Makes 4 servings*

Grilled Chicken Breasts with Zesty Peanut Sauce

1. Rinse, trim and pound chicken to ¼-inch thickness. Combine chicken and all marinade ingredients in resealable plastic food storage bag. Marinate for 1 hour or overnight in refrigerator.

2. Combine first 8 sauce ingredients in medium saucepan over medium heat. Cook for 15 minutes, stirring constantly. Whisk in broth and cream. Cook for 1 minute. Set aside.

3. Preheat grill. Remove chicken from marinade and place on hot grid. Grill for 4 to 6 minutes on each side or until center is no longer pink. Serve topped with peanut sauce.

Makes 8 servings

8 large boneless skinless chicken breast halves

Marinade
- ½ cup soy sauce
- ⅓ cup fresh lime juice
- ¼ cup CRISCO® All-Vegetable Oil*
- 2 tablespoons JIF® Creamy or Extra Crunchy Peanut Butter
- 1 tablespoon brown sugar
- 2 large cloves garlic, minced
- ½ teaspoon salt
- ½ teaspoon cayenne pepper

Sauce
- 1 cup JIF® Creamy or Extra Crunchy Peanut Butter
- 1 cup unsweetened coconut milk
- ¼ cup fresh lime juice
- 3 tablespoons soy sauce
- 2 tablespoons dark brown sugar
- 2 teaspoons minced fresh ginger
- 2 cloves garlic, minced
- ¼ teaspoon cayenne pepper, or to taste
- ½ cup chicken broth
- ½ cup heavy cream

*Or use your favorite Crisco Oil.

Hot off the Grill

Persian Chicken Breasts

1 medium lemon
2 teaspoons olive oil
1 teaspoon ground
   cinnamon
½ teaspoon salt
¼ teaspoon black pepper
¼ teaspoon turmeric
4 boneless skinless
   chicken breasts
4 flour tortillas or soft
   lavash (optional)
Grilled vegetables
   (optional)

1. Remove lemon peel in long strips with paring knife; reserve for garnish. Juice lemon; combine juice with oil, cinnamon, salt, pepper and turmeric in large heavy-duty resealable food storage bag. Gently knead ingredients in bag to mix thoroughly; add chicken. Seal bag and turn to coat thoroughly. Refrigerate 4 hours or overnight.

2. Remove chicken from marinade; gently shake to remove excess. Discard remaining marinade. Grill chicken 5 to 7 minutes per side or until chicken is no longer pink in center. Serve chicken with lightly grilled tortillas and vegetables, if desired. *Makes 4 servings*

Grilled Chicken Skewers

Spray grill grate with CRISCO Cooking Spray; heat grill. Thread chicken on skewers; grill over medium heat, turning once, 10 to 12 minutes or until cooked through. Brush with 1 cup Southern-Style Barbecue Sauce during last few minutes of cooking. Serve with remaining 1 cup sauce.

Makes 10 to 12 skewers

Prep Time: *15 minutes*
Cook Time: *1 hour, 10 to 12 minutes*

Southern-Style Barbecue Sauce

- ⅓ cup CRISCO® Vegetable Oil*
- 1 stalk celery, finely chopped
- ½ *each* red and green bell pepper, finely chopped
- 1 small onion, finely chopped
- 2 cups ketchup
- ¾ cup dark brown sugar
- ¼ cup yellow mustard
- 2 tablespoons Worcestershire sauce
- 2 tablespoons lemon juice
- 1 tablespoon garlic powder
- 1 tablespoon ground ginger
- ¾ teaspoon salt
- ½ teaspoon black pepper
- ¼ teaspoon cayenne pepper
- ¼ teaspoon chili powder

*Or use your favorite Crisco Oil.

In a large saucepan, heat CRISCO Oil over medium heat. Add celery, pepper and onion; sauté until soft. Add ketchup and sugar. Reduce heat to low; stir until sugar dissolves. Add remaining ingredients; cook on very low heat, stirring occasionally, for 1 hour.

Makes 2 cups

CRISCO® No-Stick Cooking Spray
1 pound chicken tenders
10 to 12 wooden skewers, soaked in water for 30 minutes
Southern-Style Barbecue Sauce (recipe follows)

Honey and Mustard Glazed Chicken

1 whole chicken (4 to
   5 pounds)
1 tablespoon vegetable oil
¼ cup honey
2 tablespoons Dijon
   mustard
1 tablespoon reduced-
   sodium soy sauce
½ teaspoon ground ginger
⅛ teaspoon black pepper
   Dash salt

1. Prepare grill for indirect cooking.

2. Remove giblets from chicken cavity; reserve for another use or discard. Rinse chicken with cold water; pat dry with paper towels. Pull skin over neck; secure with metal skewer. Tuck wings under back; tie legs together with wet string. Lightly brush chicken with oil.

3. Combine honey, mustard, soy sauce, ginger, pepper and salt in small bowl; set aside.

4. Place chicken, breast side up, on grid directly over drip pan.* Grill, covered, over medium-high heat 1 hour 30 minutes or until internal temperature reaches 180°F when tested with meat thermometer inserted into thickest part of thigh, not touching bone. Brush with honey mixture every 10 minutes during last 30 minutes of cooking time.

5. Transfer chicken to cutting board; cover with foil. Let stand 15 minutes before carving. Internal temperature will continue to rise 5° to 10°F during stand time. *Makes 4 to 5 servings*

*If using grill with heat on one side (rather than around drip pan), rotate chicken 180° after 45 minutes of cooking time.

Grilled Chicken and Vegetable Kabobs

1. Combine oil, lemon juice, garlic, salt, lemon pepper and tarragon in large resealable food storage bag. Add chicken, mushrooms, zucchini, bell peppers, onion and tomatoes. Seal and shake until well coated. Refrigerate at least 8 hours, turning occasionally.

2. Soak 6 (10-inch) wooden skewers in water 30 minutes; set aside.

3. Remove chicken and vegetables from marinade; discard marinade. Thread chicken and vegetables onto skewers.

4. Coat grill grid with nonstick cooking spray; place skewers on grid. Grill, covered, over medium-hot coals 3 to 4 minutes on each side or until chicken is no longer pink in center.

5. Remove chicken and vegetables from skewers and serve over rice.

Makes 6 servings

Serving Suggestion: **Serve with sliced fresh pineapple and green grapes.**

⅓ cup olive oil
¼ cup lemon juice
4 cloves garlic, coarsely chopped
½ teaspoon salt
½ teaspoon lemon pepper
½ teaspoon dried tarragon
1 pound chicken tenders
6 ounces mushrooms
1 cup sliced zucchini
½ cup cubed green bell pepper
½ cup cubed red bell pepper
1 red onion, quartered
6 cherry tomatoes
3 cups hot cooked rice

Caribbean Chutney Kabobs

20 (4-inch) bamboo
    skewers
½ medium pineapple
1 medium red bell
    pepper, cut into
    1-inch pieces
¾ pound boneless skinless
    chicken breasts, cut
    into 1-inch pieces
½ cup bottled mango
    chutney
2 tablespoons orange
    juice or pineapple
    juice
1 teaspoon vanilla
¼ teaspoon ground
    nutmeg

1. To prevent burning, soak skewers in water at least 20 minutes before assembling kabobs.

2. Peel and core pineapple. Cut half of pineapple into 1-inch chunks. Alternately thread bell pepper, pineapple and chicken onto skewers. Place in shallow baking dish.

3. Combine chutney, orange juice, vanilla and nutmeg in small bowl; mix well. Pour over kabobs; cover. Refrigerate up to 4 hours.

4. Preheat broiler. Spray broiler pan with nonstick cooking spray. Place kabobs on prepared broiler pan; discard any leftover marinade. Broil kabobs 6 to 8 inches from heat 4 to 5 minutes on each side or until chicken is no longer pink in center. Transfer to serving plates.

Makes 10 servings

Grilled Garlic Chicken

1. In medium bowl, combine soup mix with oil.

2. Add chicken; toss to coat.

3. Grill or broil until chicken is thoroughly cooked.

Makes 4 servings

1 envelope LIPTON®
  RECIPE SECRETS®
  Savory Herb with
  Garlic Soup Mix
3 tablespoons BERTOLLI®
  Olive Oil
4 boneless, skinless
  chicken breast halves
  (about 1¼ pounds)

Sizzlin' Stir-Fries

Easy Make-at-Home Chinese Chicken

3 tablespoons frozen
    orange juice
    concentrate, thawed
2 tablespoons reduced-
    sodium soy sauce
2 tablespoons water
¾ teaspoon cornstarch
¼ teaspoon garlic powder
2 carrots, peeled
    Nonstick cooking spray
1 (12-ounce) package
    broccoli and
    cauliflower florets
2 teaspoons canola oil
¾ pound boneless skinless
    chicken breasts, cut
    into bite-size pieces
1⅓ cups hot cooked rice

1. For sauce, stir together orange juice concentrate, soy sauce, water, cornstarch and garlic powder; set aside.

2. Use bottle opener or ice pick to make 4 to 5 lengthwise cuts down each carrot, being careful not to cut completely through carrot. Cut crosswise into ¼-inch-thick slices, forming flowers.

3. Spray nonstick wok or large skillet with cooking spray. Add carrots; stir-fry over high heat 1 minute. Add broccoli and cauliflower; stir-fry 2 to 3 minutes or until vegetables are crisp-tender. Remove vegetables from wok; set aside.

4. Add oil to wok. Stir-fry chicken in hot oil 2 to 3 minutes or until no longer pink in center. Push chicken up side of wok. Add sauce mixture; cook and stir until boiling. Return all vegetables to wok; cook and stir until mixture is heated through. Serve with hot cooked rice. *Makes 4 servings*

4 boneless skinless chicken breast halves (about 1½ pounds)
2 tablespoons vegetable oil
2 tablespoons orange juice
2 tablespoons light soy sauce
1 tablespoon cornstarch
1 bag (16 ounces) BIRDS EYE® frozen Farm Fresh Mixtures Broccoli, Carrots & Water Chestnuts

Chicken Stir-Fry

- Cut chicken into ½-inch-thick long strips.

- In wok or large skillet, heat oil over medium-high heat.

- Add chicken; cook 5 minutes, stirring occasionally.

- Meanwhile, in small bowl, combine orange juice, soy sauce and cornstarch; blend well and set aside.

- Add vegetables to chicken; cook 5 minutes more or until chicken is no longer pink in center, stirring occasionally.

- Stir in soy sauce mixture; cook 1 minute or until heated through.

Makes 4 servings

Serving Suggestion: Serve over hot cooked rice.

Birds Eye Idea: When cooking rice, add one teaspoon lemon juice to each quart of water you use so the grains will stay white and separate.

Prep Time: *5 minutes*
Cook Time: *12 minutes*

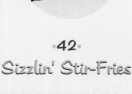

Shanghai Chicken with Asparagus and Ham

1. To blanch asparagus pieces, cook 3 minutes in enough boiling water to cover. Plunge asparagus into cold water. Drain well.

2. Heat oil in large nonstick skillet over medium heat. Add onion and garlic; stir-fry 2 minutes. Add chicken; stir-fry 2 minutes. Add asparagus; stir-fry 2 minutes or until chicken is no longer pink in center.

3. Add teriyaki sauce; mix well. Add ham; stir-fry until heated through. Serve over rice noodles. Garnish with carrot strips and fresh herbs, if desired. *Makes 4 servings*

2 cups diagonally cut 1-inch fresh asparagus pieces*
2 teaspoons vegetable oil
¾ cup coarsely chopped onion
2 cloves garlic, minced
1 pound boneless skinless chicken breasts, cut into 1-inch pieces
2 tablespoons teriyaki sauce
¼ cup diced ham
1 package(6¾ ounces) hot cooked rice noodles
Carrot strips and fresh herbs for garnish (optional)

*Or substitute thawed frozen asparagus; omit step 1.

Chicken Chow Mein

1 pound boneless skinless chicken breasts, cut into thin strips

2 cloves garlic, minced

1 teaspoon vegetable oil, divided

2 tablespoons reduced-sodium soy sauce

2 tablespoons dry sherry

6 ounces (2 cups) fresh snow peas, cut into halves

3 large green onions, cut diagonally into 1-inch pieces

4 ounces uncooked Chinese egg noodles or vermicelli, cooked, drained

1 teaspoon dark sesame oil (optional)

Cherry tomatoes for garnish (optional)

1. Toss chicken with garlic in small bowl.

2. Heat ½ teaspoon vegetable oil in wok or large nonstick skillet over medium-high heat. Add chicken mixture; stir-fry 3 minutes or until chicken is no longer pink in center. Transfer to medium bowl; toss with soy sauce and sherry.

3. Heat remaining ½ teaspoon vegetable oil in wok. Add snow peas; stir-fry 2 minutes. Add green onions; stir-fry 30 seconds. Add chicken mixture; stir-fry 1 minute.

4. Add noodles to wok; stir-fry 2 minutes or until heated through. Stir in sesame oil, if desired. Garnish with cherry tomatoes, if desired.

Makes 4 servings

Orzo with Chicken and Cabbage

1. Place 6 cups water in wok or large saucepan; bring to a boil over high heat. Add orzo; cook according to package directions until *al dente,* stirring occasionally. Drain; set aside.

2. Whisk together vinegar, chicken broth, brown sugar, soy sauce and cornstarch in small bowl; set aside.

3. Heat sesame chili oil in wok or large skillet over high heat. Add cabbage; stir-fry 2 to 3 minutes or until crisp-tender. Remove. Set aside on serving platter; keep warm.

4. Heat stir-fry oil in same wok over high heat. Add chicken; stir-fry 3 minutes or until no longer pink in center. Add snow peas and white parts of green onions; stir-fry 1 to 2 minutes or until vegetables are crisp-tender. Add vinegar mixture, stirring until hot and slightly thickened. Add orzo and cabbage; toss. Sprinkle with green onion tops and sesame seeds.

Makes 4 servings

8 ounces uncooked orzo pasta

¼ cup rice vinegar

¼ cup chicken broth

2 tablespoons packed brown sugar

2 tablespoons soy sauce

1 teaspoon cornstarch

1 tablespoon sesame chili oil

2 cups thinly sliced red cabbage

1 tablespoon seasoned stir-fry or hot oil

1 pound boneless skinless chicken breasts or tenders, cut into bite-size pieces

4 ounces snow peas

4 green onions with tops, sliced into ½-inch pieces

1 tablespoon sesame seeds, toasted

Thai Curry Stir-Fry

½ cup fat-free reduced-
   sodium chicken broth
2 teaspoons cornstarch
2 teaspoons reduced-
   sodium soy sauce
1½ teaspoons curry powder
⅛ teaspoon red pepper
   flakes
   Nonstick olive oil
   cooking spray
3 green onions, sliced
2 cloves garlic, minced
2 cups broccoli florets
⅔ cup sliced carrot
1½ teaspoons olive oil
6 ounces boneless skinless
   chicken breasts, cut
   into bite-size pieces
⅔ cup hot cooked rice,
   prepared without salt

1. Stir together broth, cornstarch, soy sauce, curry powder and red pepper flakes. Set aside.

2. Spray nonstick wok or large nonstick skillet with cooking spray. Heat over medium-high heat. Add green onions and garlic; stir-fry 1 minute. Remove from wok.

3. Add broccoli and carrot to wok; stir-fry 2 to 3 minutes or until crisp-tender. Remove from wok.

4. Add oil to hot wok. Add chicken and stir-fry 2 to 3 minutes or until no longer pink in center. Stir broth mixture; add to wok. Cook and stir until broth mixture comes to a boil and thickens slightly. Return all vegetables to wok. Heat through.

5. Serve over rice.

Makes 2 servings

Chicken and Vegetables with Mustard Sauce

1. Combine sugar, cornstarch and mustard in small bowl. Blend soy sauce, water and vinegar into cornstarch mixture until smooth. Cut chicken into 1-inch pieces.

2. Heat 2 teaspoons oil in wok or large nonstick skillet over medium heat. Add chicken and garlic; stir-fry 3 minutes or until chicken is no longer pink in center. Remove and reserve.

3. Add remaining 2 teaspoons oil to wok. Add bell pepper, celery and onion; stir-fry 3 minutes or until vegetables are crisp-tender.

4. Stir soy sauce mixture; add to wok. Cook and stir 30 seconds or until sauce boils and thickens.

5. Return chicken with any accumulated juices to wok; heat through. Serve over Chinese noodles. Garnish with celery leaves, if desired.

Makes 4 servings

1 tablespoon sugar
2 teaspoons cornstarch
1½ teaspoons dry mustard
2 tablespoons reduced-sodium soy sauce
2 tablespoons water
2 tablespoons rice vinegar
1 pound boneless skinless chicken breasts
4 teaspoons vegetable oil, divided
2 cloves garlic, minced
1 small red bell pepper, cut into short thin strips
½ cup thinly sliced celery with leaves reserved
1 small onion, cut into thin wedges
3 cups hot cooked Chinese egg noodles (3 ounces uncooked)

Golden Chicken Stir-Fry

½ pound chicken tenders, cut into thin strips

½ cup stir-fry sauce, divided

3 tablespoons vegetable oil, divided

1 medium onion, thinly sliced

1 clove garlic, minced

2 carrots, cut diagonally into thin slices

1 rib celery, cut diagonally into thin slices

1 tablespoon sesame seeds, toasted

½ teaspoon five-spice powder

¼ teaspoon dark sesame oil

2 cups hot cooked white rice

1. Toss chicken with 2 tablespoons stir-fry sauce in small bowl. Heat 1 tablespoon vegetable oil in wok or large skillet over medium-high heat. Add chicken and stir-fry 2 minutes; remove and set aside.

2. Heat remaining 2 tablespoons vegetable oil in same pan. Add onion; stir-fry 2 minutes. Add garlic, carrots and celery; stir-fry 2 minutes longer. Add remaining stir-fry sauce, chicken, sesame seeds and five-spice powder to pan. Cook and stir until chicken is no longer pink in center and vegetables are coated with sauce.

3. Remove from heat; stir in sesame oil. Serve with rice.

Makes 4 servings

Mandarin Orange Chicken

1. Combine vinegar, soy sauce, 1 tablespoon oil, orange peel and garlic in medium bowl. Add chicken; toss to coat well. Cover and refrigerate 15 minutes to 1 hour.

2. Drain chicken, reserving marinade. Drain oranges, reserving liquid; set oranges aside. Combine marinade from chicken and liquid from oranges in small bowl; add enough orange juice to make 2 cups liquid. Whisk in cornstarch and red pepper flakes; set aside.

3. Heat remaining 1 tablespoon oil in wok or large skillet over high heat. Add chicken; stir-fry 2 to 3 minutes or until no longer pink in center. Remove chicken; set aside.

4. Stir-fry onion 1 minute over high heat. Add zucchini; stir-fry 1 minute. Add bell pepper; stir-fry 1 minute or until all vegetables are crisp-tender. Add orange juice mixture. Cook and stir until mixture comes to a boil; boil 1 minute. Add chicken, cook until hot. Add oranges and gently stir. Transfer to serving plate. *Makes 6 servings*

- **2 tablespoons rice vinegar**
- **2 tablespoons light soy sauce**
- **2 tablespoons olive oil, divided**
- **2 teaspoons grated orange peel**
- **1 clove garlic, minced**
- **1 pound boneless skinless chicken breasts, cut into strips**
- **2 cans (11 ounces each) mandarin oranges, undrained**
- **½ cup orange juice**
- **2 tablespoons cornstarch**
- **½ teaspoon red pepper flakes**
- **1 onion, cut into thin wedges**
- **1 small zucchini, sliced**
- **1 red bell pepper, cut into 1-inch triangles**

Chicken and Asparagus Stir-Fry

1 cup uncooked rice
2 tablespoons vegetable oil
1 pound boneless skinless chicken breasts, cut into ½-inch-wide strips
2 medium red bell peppers, cut into thin strips
½ pound fresh asparagus,* cut diagonally into 1-inch pieces
½ cup stir-fry sauce

*For stir-frying, select thin stalks of asparagus and cut them on the diagonal—they will cook more quickly.

1. Cook rice according to package directions. Keep hot.

2. Heat oil in wok or large skillet over medium-high heat until hot. Stir-fry chicken 3 to 4 minutes or until chicken is no longer pink in center.

3. Stir in bell peppers and asparagus; reduce heat to medium. Cover and cook 2 minutes or until vegetables are crisp-tender, stirring once or twice.

4. Stir in sauce. Serve immediately with rice.   *Makes 4 servings*

Prep and Cook Time: *18 minutes*

Pineapple Basil Chicken Supreme

1. Drain pineapple, reserving juice. Combine reserved juice and cornstarch in small bowl; set aside.

2. Heat wok over high heat 1 minute. Drizzle oil into wok and heat 30 seconds. Add chicken, peppers, if desired, and garlic; stir-fry 3 minutes or until chicken is no longer pink in center. Add green onions; stir-fry 1 minute. Stir cornstarch mixture; add to wok. Cook and stir 1 minute or until thickened. Add pineapple, cashews, basil, fish sauce and soy sauce; stir-fry 1 minute or until heated through. Serve over rice and garnish, if desired.

Makes 4 servings

1 can (8 ounces) pineapple chunks in unsweetened juice
2 teaspoons cornstarch
2 tablespoons peanut oil
3 boneless skinless chicken breasts (about 1 pound), cut into ¾-inch pieces
2 to 4 serrano peppers,* cut into thin strips (optional)
2 cloves garlic, minced
2 green onions, cut into 1-inch pieces
¾ cup roasted, unsalted cashews
¼ cup chopped fresh basil
1 tablespoon fish sauce**
1 tablespoon soy sauce
Hot cooked rice
Kumquat flower for garnish

Serrano peppers can sting and irritate the skin; wear rubber gloves when handling peppers and do not touch eyes. Wash hands after handling.

**Fish sauce is available at most large supermarkets and Asian markets.*

Chicken with Walnuts

1 cup uncooked instant rice
½ cup chicken broth
¼ cup Chinese plum sauce
2 tablespoons soy sauce
2 teaspoons cornstarch
2 tablespoons vegetable oil, divided
3 cups frozen bell peppers and onions
1 pound boneless skinless chicken breasts, cut into ¼-inch strips
1 clove garlic, minced
1 cup walnut halves

1. Cook rice according to package directions.

2. Combine broth, plum sauce, soy sauce and cornstarch in small bowl; set aside.

3. Heat 1 tablespoon oil in wok or large skillet over medium-high heat Add frozen peppers and onions; stir-fry 3 minutes or until crisp-tender. Remove vegetables from wok. Drain; discard liquid.

4. Heat remaining 1 tablespoon oil in same wok. Add chicken and garlic; stir-fry 3 minutes or until chicken is no longer pink in center.

5. Stir broth mixture; add to wok. Cook and stir 1 minute or until sauce thickens. Stir in vegetables and walnuts; cook 1 minute more. Serve over rice.

Makes 4 servings

Prep and Cook Time: *19 minutes*

Sausage and Chicken Jambalaya Stir-Fry

1. Cook rice according to package directions.

2. Heat oil in wok or large skillet over medium-high heat until hot. Stir-fry chicken 2 minutes. Add sausage; stir-fry until sausage is brown and chicken is no longer pink in center, about 4 minutes. Remove from wok to medium bowl.

3. Add onion and bell pepper to wok; reduce heat to low. Cover and cook 2 to 3 minutes, stirring once or twice. Stir in garlic; cook, uncovered, 1 minute more.

4. Add tomatoes, sausage, chicken, broth, parsley, thyme, salt, black pepper and red pepper. Bring to a boil. Reduce heat to medium-low. Simmer, uncovered, 5 minutes or until most liquid has evaporated. Stir in rice; heat through. *Makes 4 servings*

Prep and Cook Time: *30 minutes*

1 cup uncooked rice
1 teaspoon vegetable oil
¼ pound chicken tenders, cut into 1-inch pieces
½ pound smoked Polish sausage, cut into bite-size pieces
1 large onion, chopped
¾ cup chopped green bell pepper
1 teaspoon bottled minced garlic
1 can (15½ ounces) diced canned tomatoes, drained
½ cup chicken broth
1 tablespoon dried parsley flakes
½ teaspoon dried thyme
¼ teaspoon salt
¼ teaspoon black pepper
⅛ to ¼ teaspoon ground red pepper

Honey Mustard BBQ Chicken Stir-Fry

1 box (10 ounces)
    couscous pasta
1 pound boneless skinless
    chicken, cut into
    strips
1 medium red bell
    pepper, cut into thin
    strips
1 medium onion, sliced
⅓ cup *French's®* Sweet &
    Tangy Honey Mustard
⅓ cup barbecue sauce

1. Prepare couscous according to package directions. Keep warm. Heat *1 tablespoon oil* in large nonstick skillet over medium-high heat. Cook and stir chicken in batches 5 to 10 minutes or until browned. Transfer to bowl. Drain fat.

2. Heat *1 tablespoon oil* in same skillet until hot. Cook and stir vegetables 3 minutes or until crisp-tender. Return chicken to skillet. Stir in *⅔ cup water,* mustard and barbecue sauce. Heat to boiling, stirring often. Serve over couscous.

Makes 4 servings

Prep Time: *10 minutes*
Cook Time: *15 minutes*

Orange Chicken Stir-Fry

Combine orange juice, 1 tablespoon oil, soy sauce, sherry, ginger, orange peel and garlic in large glass bowl. Add chicken; marinate in refrigerator 1 hour. Drain chicken, reserving marinade. Heat remaining 1 tablespoon oil in large skillet or wok over medium-high heat. Add chicken; stir-fry 3 minutes or until chicken is light brown. Add vegetables; stir-fry 3 to 5 minutes or until vegetables are crisp-tender. Combine cornstarch and marinade; add to skillet and stir until sauce boils and thickens. Stir in cashews; cook 1 minute more. Serve over hot rice.   *Makes 6 servings*

*Favorite recipe from **USA Rice Federation***

½ cup orange juice
2 tablespoons sesame oil, divided
2 tablespoons soy sauce
1 tablespoon dry sherry
2 teaspoons grated fresh ginger
1 teaspoon grated orange peel
1 clove garlic, minced
1½ pounds boneless skinless chicken breasts, cut into strips
3 cups mixed fresh vegetables, such as green bell pepper, red bell pepper, snow peas, carrots, green onions, mushrooms and/or onions
1 tablespoon cornstarch
½ cup unsalted cashew bits or halves
3 cups hot cooked rice

Sandwiches & Wraps

Blackened Chicken Salad in Pitas

1 tablespoon paprika
1 teaspoon onion powder
½ teaspoon garlic powder
½ teaspoon dried oregano
½ teaspoon dried thyme
¼ teaspoon salt
¼ teaspoon white pepper
¼ teaspoon ground red
 pepper
¼ teaspoon black pepper
2 boneless skinless
 chicken breasts
 (about ¾ pound)
4 pita bread rounds
1 cup spinach leaves, torn
 into bite-size pieces
2 small tomatoes, cut into
 8 slices
8 thin slices cucumber
½ cup prepared reduced-
 fat ranch dressing

1. Combine paprika, onion powder, garlic powder, oregano, thyme, salt and peppers in small bowl; rub on all surfaces of chicken. Grill chicken on covered grill over medium-hot coals 10 minutes per side or until chicken is no longer pink in center. Cool slightly. Cut into thin strips.

2. Wrap 2 pita bread rounds in paper towels. Microwave at HIGH 20 to 30 seconds or just until warm. Repeat with remaining pita breads. Cut in half horizontally.

3. Divide spinach, chicken strips, tomato slices, cucumber slices and ranch dressing among pita bread halves. Serve warm. *Makes 4 servings*

Chicken Tortilla Roll-Ups

4 ounces light cream
   cheese, softened
2 tablespoons mayonnaise
1 tablespoon Dijon
   mustard
¼ teaspoon black pepper
3 (10- to 12-inch) flour
   tortillas
1 cup finely chopped
   cooked chicken
¾ cup shredded or finely
   chopped carrot
¾ cup finely chopped
   green bell pepper
3 tablespoons chopped
   green onion

1. Combine cream cheese, mayonnaise, mustard and black pepper in small bowl; stir until well blended.

2. Spread cream cheese mixture evenly onto each tortilla leaving ½-inch border. Sprinkle chicken, carrot, bell pepper and onion evenly over cream cheese leaving 1½-inch border on cream cheese mixture at one end of each tortilla.

3. Roll up each tortilla jelly-roll fashion. Cut each roll into 1½-inch-thick slices. *Makes 5 to 6 appetizer servings*

Tip: Wrap rolls in plastic wrap and refrigerate for several hours for easier slicing and to allow flavors to blend.

Apricot Chicken Sandwiches

1. Drain cooked chicken; chop well. Mix with apricot spread and apricots.

2. Top bread with lettuce leaves. Divide chicken mixture evenly among bread slices; slice in half, folding over to make half-sandwich. Slice each half again to make 2 wedges. Serve immediately.　　*Makes 4 servings*

6 ounces poached
　chicken tenders
2 tablespoons apricot all-
　fruit spread
2 tablespoons chopped
　fresh apricots (pits
　removed)
4 slices whole wheat
　bread
4 lettuce leaves

Pesto Chicken & Pepper Wraps

⅔ **cup refrigerated pesto**
   sauce, divided
3 **tablespoons red wine**
   vinegar
¼ **teaspoon salt**
¼ **teaspoon black pepper**
1¼ **pounds boneless skinless**
   chicken thighs
2 **red bell peppers, cut in**
   half, stemmed and
   seeded
5 **(8-inch) flour tortillas**
5 **thin slices (3-inch**
   rounds) fresh-pack
   mozzarella cheese*
5 **leaves Boston or red**
   leaf lettuce
   Orange slices
   Red and green chilies
   Fresh basil sprigs

Packaged sliced whole milk or part-skim mozzarella cheese can be substituted.

Combine ¼ cup pesto, vinegar, salt and black pepper in medium bowl. Add chicken; toss to coat. Cover and refrigerate at least 30 minutes. Remove chicken from marinade; discard marinade. Grill chicken over medium-hot KINGSFORD® Briquets about 4 minutes per side until chicken is no longer pink in center, turning once. Grill bell peppers, skin sides down, about 8 minutes until skin is charred. Place bell peppers in large resealable plastic food storage bag; seal. Let stand 5 minutes; remove skin. Cut chicken and bell peppers into thin strips. Spread about 1 tablespoon of remaining pesto down center of each tortilla; top with chicken, bell peppers, cheese and lettuce. Roll tortillas to enclose filling. Garnish with orange slices, chilies and basil sprigs. *Makes 5 wraps*

Sandwiches & Wraps

Glazed Teriyaki Chicken Stir-Fry Sub

1. Combine mustard, teriyaki sauce, sugar substitute, ginger and vinegar in small bowl; set aside.

2. Heat oil in large skillet or wok over high heat. Stir-fry chicken 5 minutes until no longer pink. Add vegetables and stir-fry 2 minutes until just tender. Pour sauce mixture over stir-fry and cook 1 minute.

3. Arrange cabbage on rolls and top with equal portions of stir-fry. Close rolls. Serve warm.

Makes 4 servings

Prep Time: 10 minutes
Cook Time: 8 minutes

¼ cup *French's®* Honey Dijon Mustard
2 tablespoons teriyaki sauce
1 tablespoon sucralose sugar substitute
1 tablespoon grated, peeled ginger root
1 tablespoon cider or red wine vinegar
1 tablespoon vegetable oil
1 pound boneless skinless chicken breasts, cut into thin strips
1 cup coarsely chopped red or yellow bell peppers
½ cup *each* coarsely chopped red onion and plum tomatoes
4 Italian hero rolls, split (about 8 inches each)
2 cups shredded Napa cabbage or romaine lettuce

Easy Oriental Chicken Sandwiches

¼ cup peanut butter
2 tablespoons honey
2 tablespoons light soy
 sauce
½ teaspoon garlic powder
½ teaspoon ground ginger
4 boneless skinless
 chicken breasts
 (about 1¼ pounds)
4 onion or Kaiser rolls,
 split
 Lettuce leaves
1 cup sliced cucumbers
1 cup bean sprouts
¼ cup sliced green onions

1. Preheat oven to 400°F. Combine peanut butter, honey, soy sauce, garlic powder and ginger in large bowl; stir until well blended. Reserve ¼ cup peanut butter mixture.

2. Place chicken on foil-lined baking pan. Spread remaining peanut butter mixture over chicken. Bake 20 minutes or until chicken is no longer pink in center.

3. Fill rolls with lettuce, cucumbers, bean sprouts and chicken; sprinkle with green onions. Serve with reserved peanut butter mixture.

Makes 4 servings

Sandwiches & Wraps

Chicken Wraps

1. Preheat toaster oven to 350°F. Sprinkle five-spice powder over chicken thighs. Place on toaster oven tray. Bake 20 minutes or until chicken is no longer pink in center. Remove and dice chicken.

2. Place chicken in bowl. Add green onion, bean sprouts, almonds, hoisin sauce, chile sauce and soy sauce. Stir gently but well. To serve, spoon ⅓ cup chicken mixture onto each lettuce leaf; roll or fold as desired.

Makes 4 servings

½ teaspoon five-spice powder
½ pound boneless, skinless chicken thighs
2 tablespoons minced green onion
½ cup bean sprouts, rinsed well and drained
2 tablespoons sliced almonds
4 teaspoons hoisin sauce
½ tablespoon hot chile sauce with garlic*
2 tablespoons soy sauce
4 large leaves romaine or iceberg lettuce

Hot chile sauce with garlic is available in the Asian foods section of most large supermarkets.

Chicken and Mozzarella Melts

2 cloves garlic, crushed
4 boneless skinless
  chicken breasts
  (about 1 pound)
  Nonstick cooking spray
⅛ teaspoon salt
⅛ teaspoon black pepper
1 tablespoon prepared
  pesto sauce
4 small hard rolls, split
12 fresh spinach leaves
8 fresh basil leaves*
  (optional)
3 plum tomatoes, sliced
½ cup (2 ounces)
  shredded part-skim
  mozzarella cheese

*Omit basil leaves if fresh are unavailable. Do not substitute dried basil leaves.

1. Preheat oven to 350°F. Rub garlic on all surfaces of chicken. Spray medium nonstick skillet with cooking spray; heat over medium heat until hot. Add chicken; cook 5 to 6 minutes on each side or until no longer pink in center. Sprinkle with salt and pepper.

2. Brush pesto sauce onto bottom halves of rolls; layer with spinach, basil, if desired, and tomatoes. Place chicken in rolls; sprinkle cheese evenly over chicken. (If desired, sandwiches may be prepared up to this point and wrapped in aluminum foil. Refrigerate until ready to bake. Bake in preheated 350°F oven until chicken is warm, about 20 minutes.)

3. Wrap sandwiches in aluminum foil; bake about 10 minutes or until cheese is melted. *Makes 4 servings*

Asian Wraps

1. Spray nonstick wok or large skillet with cooking spray; heat over medium-high heat. Stir-fry chicken 2 minutes. Add ginger, garlic and pepper flakes; stir-fry 2 minutes. Add teriyaki sauce; mix well.* Add coleslaw mix and green onions; stir-fry 4 minutes or until chicken is no longer pink in center and coleslaw is crisp-tender.

2. Spread each tortilla with 2 teaspoons fruit spread; evenly spoon chicken mixture down center of tortillas. Roll up to form wraps.

Makes 4 servings

If sauce is too thick, add up to 2 tablespoons water to thin it.

Prep Time: *10 minutes*
Cook Time: *10 minutes*

Nonstick cooking spray
8 ounces boneless skinless chicken breasts or thighs, cut into ½-inch pieces
1 teaspoon minced fresh ginger
1 teaspoon minced fresh garlic
¼ teaspoon red pepper flakes
¼ cup reduced-sodium teriyaki sauce
4 cups (about 8 ounces) packaged coleslaw mix
½ cup sliced green onions
4 (10-inch) flour tortillas
8 teaspoons no-sugar-added plum fruit spread

Sandwiches & Wraps

Chicken, Feta and Pepper Subs

1 pound boneless, skinless chicken breasts

3 tablespoons olive oil, divided

2 teaspoons TABASCO® brand Pepper Sauce

½ teaspoon salt

½ teaspoon ground cumin

1 red bell pepper, cut into strips

1 yellow or green bell pepper, cut into strips

½ cup crumbled feta cheese

4 (6-inch) French rolls

Cut chicken breasts into thin strips. Heat 1 tablespoon oil in 12-inch skillet over medium-high heat. Add chicken; cook until well browned on all sides, stirring frequently. Stir in TABASCO® Sauce, salt and cumin. Remove mixture to medium bowl. Add remaining 2 tablespoons oil to same skillet over medium heat. Add bell peppers; cook about 5 minutes or until tender-crisp, stirring occasionally. Toss with chicken and feta cheese.

To serve, cut rolls crosswise in half. Cover bottom halves with chicken mixture and top with remaining roll halves. *Makes 4 servings*

Open-Faced Italian Focaccia Sandwich

Stir together chicken, dressing and onions in small bowl. Arrange chicken mixture evenly on top of focaccia. Top with layer of tomatoes and cheese slices. Sprinkle with Parmesan cheese, if desired. Broil 2 minutes or until cheese is melted and bubbly. *Makes 4 servings*

Note: Purchase rotisserie chicken at your favorite store to add great taste and save on preparation time.

2 cups shredded cooked chicken
½ cup HIDDEN VALLEY® The Original Ranch® Dressing
¼ cup diagonally sliced green onions
1 piece focaccia bread, about ¾-inch thick, 10×7 inches
2 medium tomatoes, thinly sliced
4 cheese slices, such as Swiss, provolone or Cheddar
2 tablespoons grated Parmesan cheese (optional)

Sandwiches & Wraps

Basil Chicken and Vegetables on Focaccia

½ cup mayonnaise
¼ teaspoon garlic powder
½ teaspoon black pepper, divided
1 loaf (16 ounces) focaccia or Italian bread
4 boneless skinless chicken breasts (about 1¼ pounds)
3 tablespoons olive oil
2 cloves garlic, minced
1½ teaspoons dried basil
½ teaspoon salt
1 green bell pepper, stemmed, seeded and cut into quarters
1 medium zucchini, cut lengthwise into 4 slices
2 Italian plum tomatoes, sliced

1. Combine mayonnaise, garlic powder and ¼ teaspoon black pepper in small bowl; set aside.

2. Cut focaccia into quarters. Cut each quarter horizontally in half; set aside.

3. Combine chicken, oil, garlic, basil, salt and remaining ¼ teaspoon black pepper in large resealable food storage bag. Seal bag; knead to combine. Add bell pepper and zucchini; knead to coat.

4. Grill or broil chicken, bell pepper and zucchini 4 inches from heat 6 to 8 minutes on each side or until chicken is no longer pink in center. (Bell pepper and zucchini may take less time.)

5. Top bottom half of each focaccia quarter with mayonnaise mixture, tomatoes, bell pepper, zucchini and chicken. Top with focaccia tops.

Makes 4 servings

Stir-Fry Pita Sandwiches

1. Cut chicken tenders in half lengthwise and crosswise. Coat large nonstick skillet with nonstick cooking spray. Cook and stir chicken over medium heat 3 minutes. Add onion and bell pepper; cook and stir 2 minutes. Add Italian dressing and red pepper flakes; cover and cook 3 minutes. Remove from heat; uncover and let cool 5 minutes.

2. While chicken mixture is cooling, cut pita breads in half to form pockets. Line each pocket with lettuce leaf. Spoon chicken filling into pockets; sprinkle with feta cheese. *Makes 4 servings*

Note: Salad dressings offer a surprising amount of convenience in the kitchen. Their basic components of oil, vinegar, herbs and spices provide a ready-made marinade or seasoned oil for cooking meats and poultry.

Prep and Cook Time: *17 minutes*

12 ounces chicken tenders
1 onion, thinly sliced
1 red bell pepper, cut into strips
½ cup zesty Italian dressing
¼ teaspoon red pepper flakes
4 pita bread rounds
8 leaves lettuce
4 tablespoons crumbled feta cheese

Mustard-Glazed Chicken Sandwiches

½ **cup honey-mustard barbecue sauce, divided**
4 Kaiser rolls, split
4 boneless skinless chicken breasts (1 pound)
4 slices Swiss cheese
4 leaves lettuce
8 slices tomato

1. Spread about 1 teaspoon barbecue sauce on cut sides of each roll.

2. Pound chicken breasts between 2 pieces of plastic wrap to ½-inch thickness with flat side of meat mallet or rolling pin. Spread remaining barbecue sauce over chicken.

3. Cook chicken in large nonstick skillet over medium-low heat 5 minutes per side or until no longer pink in center. Remove skillet from heat. Place cheese slices on chicken; let stand 3 minutes to melt.

4. Place lettuce leaves and tomato slices on roll bottoms; top with chicken and roll tops.

Makes 4 servings

Serving Suggestion: Serve sandwiches with yellow tomatoes, baby carrots and celery sticks.

Prep & Cook Time: *19 minutes*

Pita Pizzas

1. Preheat oven to 375°F. Spray medium nonstick skillet with cooking spray; heat over medium heat until hot. Add chicken; cook and stir 6 minutes or until browned and no longer pink in center. Remove chicken from skillet.

2. Spray skillet with additional cooking spray; add bell pepper, mushrooms, onion, garlic, basil and oregano. Cook and stir over medium heat 5 to 7 minutes or until vegetables are crisp-tender. Return chicken to skillet; stir well.

3. Place spinach on top of pita breads. Divide chicken and vegetable mixture evenly; spoon over spinach. Sprinkle evenly with mozzarella and Parmesan cheese. Bake, uncovered, 7 to 10 minutes or until cheese is melted. *Makes 6 servings*

Nonstick cooking spray
½ pound boneless skinless chicken breasts, cut into ½-inch cubes
½ cup *each* thinly sliced red bell pepper and mushrooms
½ cup thinly sliced red onion (about 1 small)
2 cloves garlic, minced
1 teaspoon dried basil
½ teaspoon dried oregano
1 cup torn fresh spinach leaves
6 mini whole wheat pita breads
½ cup (2 ounces) shredded part-skim mozzarella cheese
1 tablespoon grated Parmesan cheese

Chicken and Pear Pita Pockets

3 cups diced cooked
chicken
1 can (16 ounces) Bartlett
Pear halves or slices,
thoroughly drained
and diced
¾ cup chopped celery
½ cup raisins or chopped
dates
¼ cup *each* nonfat plain
yogurt and lowfat
mayonnaise
1 teaspoon *each* salt,
lemon pepper and
dried rosemary
6 pita pocket breads,
halved
12 lettuce leaves

Combine chicken, pears, celery and raisins in medium bowl. Prepare dressing by blending yogurt, mayonnaise, salt, lemon pepper and rosemary. Combine dressing and pear mixture; mix well. Refrigerate until serving. To serve, line each pita half with lettuce leaf. Portion ½ cup mixture into each half.

Makes 6 servings

Favorite recipe from **Pacific Northwest Canned Pear Service**

Walnut Chicken Salad Sandwich

In large bowl, combine yogurt, celery, spinach, onion, lemon juice, mustard and dill. Stir in chicken, apple and walnuts. Season with salt and pepper, if desired. Spoon ½ cup salad into each pita bread half; tuck in lettuce leaf.

Makes 4 sandwiches

*Favorite recipe from **Walnut Marketing Board***

⅔ **cup nonfat plain yogurt**
½ **cup *each* finely chopped celery and fresh spinach**
¼ **cup chopped green onion**
1 **tablespoon lemon juice**
1 **teaspoon ground mustard**
1 **tablespoon chopped fresh dill**
3 **cups diced cooked chicken breasts**
1 **apple, cored and diced**
½ **cup (2 ounces) chopped California walnuts**
Salt and black pepper (optional)
4 **pita breads, halved**
4 **iceberg lettuce leaves or other crisp lettuce leaves**

Cozy Casseroles

Chicken, Asparagus & Mushroom Bake

1 tablespoon butter
1 tablespoon olive oil
2 boneless skinless
    chicken breasts
    (about ½ pound), cut
    into bite-size pieces
2 cloves garlic, minced
1 cup sliced mushrooms
2 cups sliced asparagus
    Black pepper
1 package (about
    6 ounces) corn bread
    stuffing mix
¼ cup dry white wine
1 can (14½ ounces)
    chicken broth
1 can (10½ ounces)
    condensed low-
    sodium condensed
    cream of chicken
    soup, undiluted

1. Preheat oven to 350°F. Heat butter and oil in large skillet until butter is melted. Cook and stir chicken and garlic about 3 minutes over medium-high heat until chicken is no longer pink in center. Add mushrooms; cook and stir 2 minutes. Add asparagus; cook and stir about 5 minutes or until asparagus is crisp-tender. Season with pepper.

2. Transfer mixture to 2½-quart casserole or 6 small casseroles. Top with stuffing mix.

3. Add wine to skillet, if desired; cook and stir 1 minute over medium-high heat, scraping up any browned bits from bottom of skillet. Add broth and soup; cook and stir until well blended.

4. Pour broth mixture into casserole; mix well. Bake, uncovered, about 35 minutes (30 minutes for small casseroles) or until heated through and lightly browned.
Makes 6 servings

Tip: This is a good way to stretch a little leftover chicken into an easy and tasty dinner. Serve with a tossed green salad and sliced tomatoes.

Spicy Chicken Casserole with Corn Bread

2 tablespoons olive oil
4 boneless skinless chicken breasts, cut into bite-size pieces
1 envelope (about 1 ounce) taco seasoning
1 can (about 15 ounces) black beans, rinsed and drained
1 can (14½ ounces) diced tomatoes, drained
1 can (about 10 ounces) Mexican-style corn, drained
1 can (about 4 ounces) diced green chiles, drained
½ cup mild salsa
1 box (about 8½ ounces) corn bread mix, plus ingredients to prepare
½ cup (2 ounces) shredded Cheddar cheese
¼ cup chopped red bell pepper

1. Preheat oven to 350°F. Spray 2-quart casserole with nonstick cooking spray. Set aside. Heat oil in large skillet over medium heat. Cook chicken until no longer pink in center.

2. Sprinkle taco seasoning over chicken. Add black beans, tomatoes, corn, chiles and salsa; stir until well blended. Transfer to prepared dish.

3. Prepare corn bread mix according to package directions, adding cheese and bell pepper. Spread batter over chicken mixture.

4. Bake 30 minutes or until corn bread is golden brown.

Makes 4 to 6 servings

Cozy Casseroles

Chicken and Black Bean Enchiladas

Preheat oven to 350°F. Grease 15×10-inch jelly-roll baking pan. Combine picante sauce, cilantro, chili powder and cumin in large saucepan. Bring to a boil. Reduce heat to low; simmer 5 minutes.

Combine 1½ cups sauce mixture, chicken, beans and ⅔ *cup* French Fried Onions in medium bowl. Spoon a scant ½ cup filling over bottom third of each tortilla. Roll up tortillas enclosing filling and arrange, seam-side down, in a single layer in bottom of prepared baking pan. Spoon remaining sauce evenly over tortillas.

Bake, uncovered, 20 minutes or until heated through. Sprinkle with remaining ⅔ *cup* onions and cheese. Bake 5 minutes or until cheese is melted and onions are golden. Serve immediately.

Makes 5 to 6 servings (4 cups sauce, 4½ cups filling)

Tip: This is a great make-ahead party dish.

Prep Time: *45 minutes*
Cook Time: *25 minutes*

2 jars (16 ounces each) mild picante sauce
¼ cup chopped fresh cilantro
2 tablespoons chili powder
1 teaspoon ground cumin
2 cups (10 ounces) chopped cooked chicken
1 can (15 ounces) black beans, drained and rinsed
1⅓ cups *French's®* French Fried Onions, divided
1 package (about 10 ounces) flour tortillas (7 inches)
1 cup (4 ounces) shredded Monterey Jack cheese with jalapeño peppers

Bayou-Style Pot Pie

1 tablespoon olive oil
1 large onion, chopped
1 green bell pepper, chopped
1½ teaspoons minced garlic
½ pound boneless skinless chicken thighs, cut into 1-inch pieces
1 can (14½ ounces) stewed tomatoes
½ pound fully cooked smoked sausage or kielbasa, thinly sliced
¾ teaspoon hot pepper sauce, or to taste
2¼ cups buttermilk baking mix
¾ teaspoon dried thyme
⅛ teaspoon black pepper
⅔ cup milk

1. Preheat oven to 450°F. Heat oil in medium ovenproof skillet over medium-high heat until hot. Add onion, bell pepper and garlic. Cook 3 minutes, stirring occasionally.

2. Add chicken and cook 1 minute. Add tomatoes, sausage and hot pepper sauce. Cook, uncovered, over medium-low heat 5 minutes.

3. While chicken is cooking, combine baking mix, thyme and black pepper. Stir in milk. Drop batter by heaping tablespoonfuls in mounds over chicken mixture. Bake 14 minutes or until biscuits are golden brown and cooked through and chicken mixture is bubbly.

Makes 4 servings

Note: You can use any variety of fully cooked sausages from your supermarket meat case. Andouille, a fairly spicy Louisiana-style sausage, is perfect for this dish.

Prep and Cook Time: *28 minutes*

Stewed Tomatoes

Chicken Normandy Style

1. Preheat oven to 350°F. Grease 9-inch square casserole dish.

2. Melt 1 tablespoon butter in 12-inch nonstick skillet. Add apple slices; cook and stir over medium heat 7 to 10 minutes or until tender. Remove apple slices from skillet.

3. Add ground chicken to same skillet; brown over medium heat, stirring to break up meat. Drain fat. Stir in apple brandy and cook 2 minutes. Stir in soup, green onions, sage, pepper and apple slices. Simmer 5 minutes.

4. Toss noodles with remaining 1 tablespoon butter. Spoon into prepared casserole. Top with chicken mixture. Bake 15 minutes or until hot.

Makes 4 servings

2 tablespoons butter, divided

3 cups peeled, thinly sliced apples, such as Fuji or Braeburn (about 3 apples)

1 pound ground chicken

¼ cup apple brandy or apple juice

1 can (10¾ ounces) condensed cream of chicken soup, undiluted

¼ cup finely chopped green onions (green part only)

2 teaspoons fresh minced sage *or* ½ teaspoon dried sage

¼ teaspoon black pepper

1 package (12 ounces) egg noodles, cooked and drained

Chicken-Asparagus Casserole

2 teaspoons vegetable oil
1 cup seeded and chopped
   green bell pepper
1 medium onion, chopped
2 cloves garlic, minced
1 can (10¾ ounces)
   condensed cream of
   asparagus soup,
   undiluted
1 container (8 ounces)
   ricotta cheese
2 cups (8 ounces)
   shredded Cheddar
   cheese, divided
2 eggs
1½ cups chopped cooked
   chicken
1 package (10 ounces)
   frozen chopped
   asparagus, thawed
   and drained
8 ounces egg noodles,
   cooked

1. Preheat oven to 350°F. Grease 13×9-inch casserole; set aside.

2. Heat oil in small skillet over medium heat. Add bell peppers, onion and garlic; cook and stir until vegetables are crisp-tender.

3. Mix soup, ricotta cheese, 1 cup Cheddar cheese and eggs in large bowl until well blended. Add onion mixture, chicken, asparagus and noodles; mix well.

4. Spread mixture evenly in prepared casserole. Top with remaining 1 cup Cheddar cheese.

5. Bake 30 minutes or until center is set and cheese is bubbly. Let stand 5 minutes before serving. Garnish as desired. *Makes 12 servings*

Cozy Casseroles

Apple Curry Chicken

1. Preheat oven to 350°F. Lightly grease 2-quart round baking dish.

2. Arrange chicken breasts in single layer in prepared dish.

3. Combine ¼ cup apple juice, salt and pepper in small bowl. Pour juice mixture over chicken.

4. Combine croutons, apple, onion, raisins, brown sugar, curry powder, poultry seasoning and garlic powder in large bowl. Stir into remaining ¾ cup apple juice.

5. Spread crouton mixture over chicken. Cover with foil; bake 45 minutes or until chicken is tender and no longer pink in center. Garnish, if desired.   *Makes 4 servings*

**4 boneless skinless
  chicken breasts**
1 cup apple juice, divided
¼ teaspoon salt
  Dash black pepper
1½ cups plain croutons
1 medium apple, chopped
1 medium onion, chopped
¼ cup raisins
2 teaspoons brown sugar
1 teaspoon curry powder
**¾ teaspoon poultry
  seasoning**
⅛ teaspoon garlic powder
**2 slices apple and fresh
  sprigs of thyme for
  garnish (optional)**

Chicken & Biscuits

¼ cup (½ stick) butter or margarine

4 boneless skinless chicken breasts (about 1¼ pounds), cut into ½-inch pieces

½ cup chopped onion

½ teaspoon dried thyme

½ teaspoon paprika

¼ teaspoon black pepper

1 can (about 14 ounces) chicken broth, divided

⅓ cup all-purpose flour

1 package (10 ounces) frozen peas and carrots

1 can (12 ounces) refrigerated biscuits

1. Preheat oven to 375°F. Melt butter in large skillet over medium heat. Add chicken, onion, thyme, paprika and pepper. Cook 5 minutes or until chicken is no longer pink in center.

2. Combine ¼ cup chicken broth with flour in small bowl; stir until smooth. Set aside.

3. Add remaining chicken broth to skillet; bring to a boil. Gradually add flour mixture, stirring constantly to prevent lumps from forming. Simmer 5 minutes. Add peas and carrots; continue cooking 2 minutes.

4. Transfer mixture to 1½-quart casserole; top with biscuits. Bake 25 to 30 minutes or until biscuits are golden brown.

Makes 4 to 6 servings

Tip: Cook the chicken in an ovenproof skillet, instead of the 1½-quart casserole. Place the biscuits directly on the chicken and vegetable mixture, then bake as directed.

Heartland Chicken Casserole

1. Preheat oven to 350°F.

2. Combine bread cubes and 1 cup cracker crumbs in large mixing bowl. Add chicken, broth, onion, celery, mushrooms, pimientos and eggs; mix well. Season with salt and pepper; spoon into 2½-quart casserole.

3. Melt margarine in small saucepan. Add remaining ½ cup cracker crumbs and brown, stirring occasionally. Sprinkle crumbs over casserole.

4. Bake 1 hour or until hot and bubbly.   *Makes 6 servings*

10 slices white bread, cubed
1½ cups cracker or dry bread crumbs, divided
4 cups cubed cooked chicken
3 cups chicken broth
1 cup chopped onion
1 cup chopped celery
1 can (8 ounces) sliced mushrooms, drained
1 jar (about 4 ounces) pimientos, diced
3 eggs, lightly beaten
Salt and black pepper
1 tablespoon margarine

Cozy Casseroles

Classic Veg•All® Chicken Pot Pie

2 cans (15 ounces each) VEG•ALL® Original Mixed Vegetables, drained
1 can (10 ounces) cooked chicken, drained
1 can (10¾ ounces) cream of chicken soup
¼ teaspoon thyme
¼ teaspoon pepper
2 (9-inch) frozen ready-to-bake pie crust

1. Preheat oven to 375°F. In medium bowl, combine Veg•All, chicken, soup, thyme and pepper; mix well. Fit one pie crust into 9-inch pie pan; pour vegetable mixture into pie crust. Top with remaining crust; crimp edges to seal and prick top with fork.

2. Bake for 30 to 45 minutes (on lower rack) or until crust is golden brown and filling is hot. Allow pie to cool slightly before cutting into wedges to serve.   *Makes 4 servings*

Cozy Casseroles

Easy Chicken Chalupas

1. Preheat oven to 350°F. Spray 13×9-inch ovenproof dish with cooking spray.

2. Remove skin and bones from chicken; discard. Shred chicken meat.

3. Place 2 tortillas in bottom of prepared dish, overlapping slightly. Layer tortillas with 1 cup chicken, ½ cup cheese and ¼ cup of each salsa. Repeat layers, ending with cheese and salsas.

4. Bake casserole 25 minutes or until bubbly and hot.

Makes 6 servings

Tip: Serve this easy main dish with some custom toppings on the side such as sour cream, chopped cilantro, sliced black olives (pre-sliced from a can, of course!) and sliced avocado.

1 roasted chicken (about 2 pounds)
8 flour tortillas
2 cups reduced-fat shredded Cheddar cheese
1 cup mild green chili salsa
1 cup mild red salsa

Cheesy Chicken Enchiladas

¼ cup (½ stick) butter
1 cup chopped onion
2 cloves garlic, minced
¼ cup all-purpose flour
1 cup chicken broth
4 ounces cream cheese, softened
2 cups (8 ounces) shredded Mexican cheese blend, divided
1 cup shredded cooked chicken
1 can (7 ounces) chopped green chilies, drained
½ cup diced pimientos
6 (8-inch) flour tortillas, warmed
¼ cup chopped fresh cilantro
¾ cup prepared salsa

1. Preheat oven to 350°F. Spray 13×9-inch baking dish with nonstick cooking spray.

2. Melt butter in medium saucepan over medium heat. Add onion and garlic; cook and stir until onion is tender. Add flour; cook and stir 1 minute. Gradually whisk in chicken broth; cook and stir 2 to 3 minutes or until slightly thickened. Add cream cheese; stir until melted. Stir in ½ cup shredded cheese, chicken, chilies and pimientos.

3. Spoon about ⅓ cup mixture onto each tortilla. Roll up; place, seam side down, in prepared baking dish. Pour remaining mixture over enchiladas; sprinkle with remaining 1½ cups shredded cheese.

4. Bake 20 minutes or until bubbly and lightly browned. Sprinkle with cilantro and serve with salsa. *Makes 6 servings*

One-Crust Chicken Pot Pie

Preheat oven to 425°F. In a 2-quart saucepan, melt CRISCO Shortening; add onion and cook until translucent. Add all-purpose baking mix. Add salt, pepper and thyme, stirring constantly. Add broth, then milk; bring to a slow, low boil. Add vegetables and chicken; keep over low heat while preparing crust.

For crust, mix all-purpose baking mix with water and CRISCO Shortening. Pat out dough onto waxed paper; roll the crust to fit the dish you are using. The crust should be fairly thick. Carefully pour the filling into the baking dish. Fit the crust on top of the mixture; make slits for steam to escape. Bake for 25 to 30 minutes or until crust is lightly browned.

Makes 4 to 6 servings

Prep Time: *25 minutes*
Cook Time: *25 to 30 minutes*

⅓ **CRISCO® Butter Flavor Stick or ⅓ cup CRISCO® Butter Flavor Shortening**
⅓ **cup chopped onion**
½ **cup all-purpose baking mix**
½ **teaspoon salt**
¼ **teaspoon pepper**
⅛ **teaspoon thyme**
1½ **cups chicken broth (homemade or canned)**
⅔ **cup milk (add 4 tablespoons PET® Evaporated Milk for a richer taste)**
1½ **cups frozen mixed vegetables**
1¾ **cups cooked chicken, chopped**

Crust
2 **cups all-purpose baking mix**
4 **tablespoons warm water**
¼ **CRISCO® Butter Flavor Stick or ¼ cup CRISCO® Butter Flavor Shortening**

Chicken & Rice Bake

1 can (10¾ ounces)
    condensed cream of
    mushroom soup
1¾ cups water
1½ cups sliced mushrooms
 ¾ cup uncooked long-
    grain rice
1⅓ cups *French's®* French
    Fried Onions, divided
 4 teaspoons *French's®*
    Worcestershire Sauce,
    divided
 4 chicken breast halves
    (about 2 pounds)
 ½ teaspoon *each* paprika
    and dried thyme

Preheat oven to 375°F. Combine soup, water, mushrooms, rice, ⅔ *cup* French Fried Onions and 2 teaspoons Worcestershire in 3-quart oblong baking dish. Arrange chicken over rice mixture. Brush chicken with remaining Worcestershire and sprinkle with paprika and thyme.

Bake, uncovered, 1 hour or until chicken is no longer pink in center. Top with remaining ⅔ *cup* onions. Bake 3 minutes or until onions are golden.

Makes 4 servings

Tip: Remove skin from chicken before baking, if desired.

Prep Time: *10 minutes*
Cook Time: *about 1 hour*

Cozy Casseroles

Artichoke-Olive Chicken Bake

1. Preheat oven to 350°F. Spray 2-quart casserole with nonstick cooking spray.

2. Cook pasta according to package directions until al dente. Drain.

3. Heat oil in large deep skillet over medium heat until hot. Add onion and pepper; cook and stir 1 minute. Add pasta, chicken, tomatoes with juice, artichokes, olives and Italian seasoning; mix until blended.

4. Place half of chicken mixture in prepared dish; sprinkle with half of cheese. Top with remaining chicken mixture and remaining cheese.

5. Bake, covered, 35 minutes or until hot and bubbly.

Makes 8 servings

1½ cups uncooked rotini
1 tablespoon olive oil
1 medium onion, chopped
½ green bell pepper, chopped
2 cups shredded cooked chicken
1 can (14½ ounces) diced tomatoes with Italian-style herbs, undrained
1 can (14 ounces) artichoke hearts, drained and quartered
1 can (6 ounces) sliced black olives, drained
1 teaspoon dried Italian seasoning
2 cups (8 ounces) shredded mozzarella cheese

Cozy Casseroles

Chicken Vera Cruz

1 chicken (3 pounds), cut up

1 jar (12 ounces) salsa

1⅓ cups *French's*® French Fried Onions, divided

½ cup Spanish stuffed olives, sliced

½ cup beer or nonalcoholic malt beverage

2 tablespoons lemon juice

2 tablespoons chopped fresh parsley *or* 1 tablespoon dried parsley

¼ teaspoon ground black pepper

Cooked white rice (optional)

Preheat oven to 350°F. Place chicken in 2-quart shallow dish. Bake, uncovered, 40 minutes. Drain.

Combine salsa, ⅔ *cup* French Fried Onions, olives, beer, lemon juice, parsley and pepper in medium saucepan. Bring to a boil. Reduce heat to low. Cook and stir 5 minutes or until slightly thickened. Pour sauce over chicken. Bake 15 minutes or until chicken is no longer pink near bone. Sprinkle with remaining ⅔ *cup* onions. Bake 5 minutes or until onions are golden. Serve with rice, if desired.   *Makes 4 to 6 servings*

Prep Time: *15 minutes*
Cook Time: *60 minutes*

Acknowledgments

The publisher would like to thank the companies and organizations listed below for the use of their recipes and photographs in this publication.

Birds Eye Foods

Crisco is a registered trademark of The J.M. Smucker Company

Del Monte Corporation

The Hidden Valley® Food Products Company

The Kingsford® Products Co.

Lawry's® Foods

McIlhenny Company (TABASCO® brand Pepper Sauce)

Pacific Northwest Canned Pear Service

Reckitt Benckiser Inc.

Unilever Foods North America

USA Rice Federation

Veg•All®

Walnut Marketing Board

Index

Metric Conversion Chart

VOLUME MEASUREMENTS (dry)

1/8 teaspoon = 0.5 mL
1/4 teaspoon = 1 mL
1/2 teaspoon = 2 mL
3/4 teaspoon = 4 mL
1 teaspoon = 5 mL
1 tablespoon = 15 mL
2 tablespoons = 30 mL
1/4 cup = 60 mL
1/3 cup = 75 mL
1/2 cup = 125 mL
2/3 cup = 150 mL
3/4 cup = 175 mL
1 cup = 250 mL
2 cups = 1 pint = 500 mL
3 cups = 750 mL
4 cups = 1 quart = 1 L

VOLUME MEASUREMENTS (fluid)

1 fluid ounce (2 tablespoons) = 30 mL
4 fluid ounces (1/2 cup) = 125 mL
8 fluid ounces (1 cup) = 250 mL
12 fluid ounces (1 1/2 cups) = 375 mL
16 fluid ounces (2 cups) = 500 mL

WEIGHTS (mass)

1/2 ounce = 15 g
1 ounce = 30 g
3 ounces = 90 g
4 ounces = 120 g
8 ounces = 225 g
10 ounces = 285 g
12 ounces = 360 g
16 ounces = 1 pound = 450 g

DIMENSIONS

1/16 inch = 2 mm
1/8 inch = 3 mm
1/4 inch = 6 mm
1/2 inch = 1.5 cm
3/4 inch = 2 cm
1 inch = 2.5 cm

OVEN TEMPERATURES

250°F = 120°C
275°F = 140°C
300°F = 150°C
325°F = 160°C
350°F = 180°C
375°F = 190°C
400°F = 200°C
425°F = 220°C
450°F = 230°C

BAKING PAN SIZES

Utensil	Size in Inches/Quarts	Metric Volume	Size in Centimeters
Baking or Cake Pan (square or rectangular)	8×8×2	2 L	20×20×5
	9×9×2	2.5 L	23×23×5
	12×8×2	3 L	30×20×5
	13×9×2	3.5 L	33×23×5
Loaf Pan	8×4×3	1.5 L	20×10×7
	9×5×3	2 L	23×13×7
Round Layer Cake Pan	8×1½	1.2 L	20×4
	9×1½	1.5 L	23×4
Pie Plate	8×1¼	750 mL	20×3
	9×1¼	1 L	23×3
Baking Dish or Casserole	1 quart	1 L	—
	1½ quart	1.5 L	—
	2 quart	2 L	—